November 1992

AF270913

Dear Joan:

You are really one who knows my mind.

Good reading

Fondly

Jerry

Jerrold E. Baker

Read My Mind

Read My Mind

Jerrold E. Baker

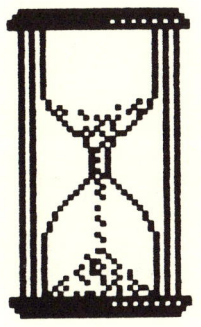

VANTAGE PRESS
New York

Published by Vantage Press, Inc.
516 West 34th Street, New York, New York 10001

Manufactured in the United States of America
ISBN: 0-533-10283-9

Library of Congress Catalog Card No.: 92-90750

0 9 8 7 6 5 4 3 2 1

This book is lovingly dedicated to my best friend, partner in life, and source of inspiration to me, our children, and our grandchildren . . . Penny Baker

Contents

Section B: Select Poems

Section C: Select Essays

Preface

With my recognizable memory dating back to the first seven months of my life, I am cognizant mine is a very inquisitive mind. When I prepared a genealogical story about my family, it was my mother (with whom I wasn't raised) and her boyfriend of forty years, Michael J. Ryan, who were shocked by my recall. They were the ones who documented the precise beginnings of my awareness in this world.

Recalling the difficult times and experiences of my early years, I came to accept many things the hard way. A good example concerns my foster mother, Mrs. Walter Kineavy, now deceased, of Prospect Park, Pennsylvania. She was the very first person who recognized that I carried an intuitive belief that there was nothing I couldn't do. Often she was exasperated by my proclamation: "I can do that." Such was a claim at seven that I could swim. I had never been in a body of water, let alone a swimming pool, but I asserted I could swim. The truth is I couldn't swim. And I have never been a good swimmer.

What is more important here is that I believed I could. I didn't wish to accept any humiliation or defeat. The very least I could do was learn—especially if others could do it.

That belief in myself, cocky perhaps for a seven-year-old, has nonetheless permeated my thinking. All that is necessary is to put one's mind to work, one's physical body to the task, or one's education to the rudiments.

I suspect the outgrowth from those early experiences was to examine and postulate more often on the things I did not understand or the things unknown to man in general.

My life has been abundant with ideas and creative excursions. The makeup of my genes can probably be tagged as the source, although I have referred to these more frequently as "gifts." Rightfully, I would say that is a simple but accurate statement.

Following the conclusion of my weekly radio broadcasts on KUCR-FM, in Riverside, California, in 1985, I set about preparing another series of programs. I titled this effort "Insights with Dorrej Rekab." Dorrej Rekab was a pseudonym I had established for myself. I merely knocked the "L" out of my first name, Jerrold—and turned the rest backward to form Dorrej. Rekab backward is Baker.

Using various essays from my sizable inventory, I narrated them to a musical background. They were designed in the Galen Drake formula of radio from the 1940s and were to run for approximately ten minutes of air time each. I submitted a dozen of these to the manager of the radio station. He thought they were excellent. However, in his opinion the stories could not be worked into their tight schedules.

Before giving up on the idea, I asked an acquaintance to listen to them and give me his opinion. He agreed. Several days later, he returned with the audio tapes. I was anxious to hear his comments, but in no way prepared for what happened.

"Jerry," he said, "who the hell do you think you are, Jesus Christ?"

I was shocked. I couldn't understand why he equated Jesus Christ with my writings, and I asked him to explain what he meant.

"In the first place, you didn't even go to college. And in the second place, you pontificate as if you were an authority on every subject."

He was red in the face, shaking, and visibly disturbed. "Mad" is the more accurate portrayal. But before he continued, I interrupted. "Ken, let me first say that the outcome of anyone's education, regardless of whether or not he went to college, is learning or, more accurately, a confidence in understanding from one's experiences, studies, and observations."

His mouth opened to talk, but I held the floor and continued. "By the way, tell me, Ken, what college Jesus graduated from, will you?"

"That's a different matter," he grumbled. "Jesus didn't have to go to college."

Without relating the continuing exchange of views between us, suffice it to say I felt there was some message in the man's religious awareness that prevented him from believing all men can achieve knowledge and understanding regardless of what degrees they may or may not hold. I did find the experience sufficient reason at the time to put the whole concept on the shelf.

Largely, the scope of this book deals with perceptions I have acquired over the years from my education and experiences—not forgetting, of course, my powers of observation.

Read My Mind, therefore, is a sampling of one man's creative excursions.

Read My Mind

Section A
Gems of Wisdom

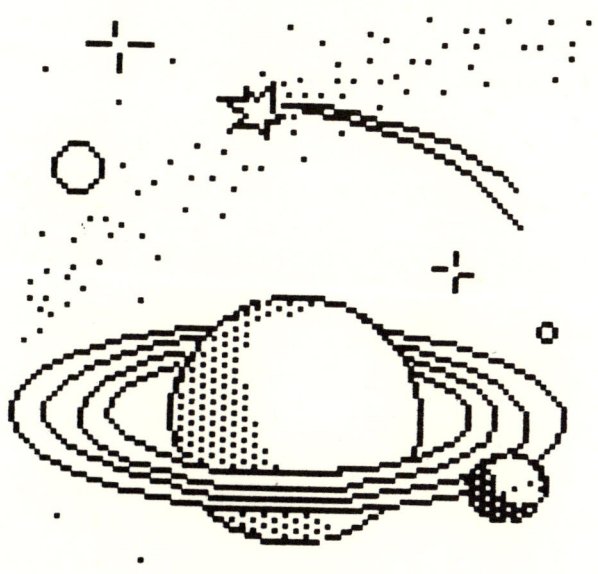

Introductory Remarks

The dictionary defines a *quotation* as "a passage referred to, repeated, or adduced." *Adduced,* I suppose, comes closest to conquering the meaning of what I call, in this section, "Gems of Wisdom."

Most of the gems of wisdom printed in this volume have been gleaned from passages of various essays written through the years. Some have come from poems and others still from single thought processes.

I have selected what I believe to be the very best of my quotations, and I would be intensely gratified if their value finds a place in people's thought processes.

I don't present them as a scripture for living. However, I do offer them as a means to unplug blockages in the brain, in order to gain new perspective.

A Quandary

I often wonder if man is
Condemned
More by what he does in his life,
As opposed to what he doesn't
Do
With his life.

Age

Age consciousness
And
Discrimination
Are bastions
Of
Perfidious behavior.

An Experience

Sometimes,
An experience people fear the
Most
Is, in all probability,
An experience they need
To confront the most.

Assignment

God is blamed
And credited
For more things
Than seems logical.

Being Free

Being free is having
The freedom
To
Change one's mind.

Birth and Death

Life is composed of
What happens
Between two opposites:
Birth and death.

Change

Change in our world
Is absolute and easy to envision,
Yet paradoxically,
It is the hardest to accept.

Coincidence

A coincidence is strictly
A pseudonym
For a reality
We don't understand.

Comment on Sales

You don't save
By spending.
You save by
Not spending.

Compassion

Compassion is the ability
To comprehend need;
The understanding,
Desire,
And love
To address need.

Confrontation

Real pride and honor
Come from confronting reality,
Seeking truth,
Then
Embracing it with
Understanding, love, and
Compassion.

Confusion

Somewhere amid the debris
Of physical and spiritual laws,
Man eludes the reality
Of his
Dual nature.

Counterfeit

In order to counterfeit
Something
You need the original
To copy.

Definition of Fear

Fear is nothing more
Than
Imagination gone rampant
Or
Experience gone starved.

Destruction

When man destroys,
He is setting a force in motion
To destroy himself as well.

Dreams

Dreams are the filing cabinet
For
Our frustrations,
Our insecurities,
And our perceived guilt.

Earth

Earth cannot survive
With either
Total peace or total war.
Duality is
Its umbilical cord.

Economics

Today's citizens
Owe much and own little.
They should own much
And owe little.

Education

Having an education
Doesn't guarantee progress
Any more than
Having progress
Guarantees an education.

Facts

**Facts support the truth.
They cannot do the same
For a lie.**

Fiction

Man's proclivity to fiction
Is escapism from
Reality
And
Fact.

Genius

Genius
From my vantage point
Seems to be
As much part-time
As it is full time.

Giving

Sometimes,
It is nice to be remembered
Not so much for what you can
Give,
But more
For what you have given.

Good and Bad

Good and bad
Are perceptions
Of
The human ego.

Happiness

Happiness is being satisfied
With all the things you have
And content in being without
All the things you don't have.

Honor

Honor today is being
Supplanted
By the shallow facade of the ego
And
The gratification of self.

Hunger

Hunger, with all its facets,
Is one of the primary
Driving forces
In life.

Imagery

A physical counterpart
Must have
A spiritual prototype.

Inner Voice

Listen to your desires.
Cling to your drives.
Enjoy your dreams.
They are the mold from which
All the world was created.
And
They are the mark of an
Achiever.

Judgment

Man must be judged both by
What he does in his life
And by
What he doesn't do with his life.

Justice

Justice in our country
Is becoming an enigma.
It is seldom just,
Rarely swift,
And never inexpensive.

Learning

Man's capacity to learn
Is limited in proportion
To his determination to seek,
His desire to achieve,
And his dedication to detail.

Life, Love, and Death

Life is a teaching experience.
Love is a learning experience.
Graduation from them
Is a spiritual experience.

Love

To be loved,
One must give of love.

Man's Preoccupation

Man's preoccupation with
Himself
Brings about a lack of symmetry
With nature.
Too often, he forgets he is a
Part of it,
Certainly not the master.

Man's Senses

Because man believes what
He wants to believe,
Hears what he wants to hear,
He imprisons his senses.

Ministers

I don't believe
All the ministers of God
Are in the pulpit.

Nature of Life

By man's inability to equate
His life with nature,
The nature of life
Is rarely equated.

Order of Things

Man is bound by his mistakes,
Guided by his deeds,
Elevated by his sacrifice,
And, most important,
Redeemed by his
Love.

Outlook

Man must fathom his
Finite nature
Against the infinite
He surveys.

Past versus Present

Americans seem to have
Elevated
To a place of reverence
All things previous civilizations
Considered an abomination.

People

People are envious of
Determination.
They are leery of
Motivation.
And all too often they
Are downright jealous of
Inspiration.

Point of View

Not everything we consider bad
Is evil.
Not everything we call good
Is right.
The sun doesn't always light
Our days,
Nor the darkness shroud our
Every night.

Problems

All men are subject
To problems
In the proportion
They are
Capable of surmounting.

Progress

Progress is one of,
If not the most,
Overstated words
In the
English language.

Question

Is the road to hell paved more
By
Honest people who weren't
Very smart?
Or by
Smart people who weren't
Very honest?

Reality

Man is still infantile
In the heavens.
He is no more than a
Microcosm of
The universe.

Religious Views

The world sees more of
Religious bigotry
Than it does of
Religious tolerance.

Right and Wrong

Being all right or all wrong
Is incompatible
With living
On earth.

Shortcoming

It seems that all too many
People
Place heavy emphasis
On the hereafter
And too little concern
With the herein.

Silence

Silence
Is a form of noise,
As noise
Can be a form of silence.

Spaceman

Man is a traveler
In space,
But he is an inhabitant
Of earth.

Survival

All forms of life on earth
Are encapsulated
In its very destiny.

Technology

Technology ushers in
New ideas, new truths,
New experiences,
New questions,
And
New answers.

The Achievable

None of us should be so blinded
By our achievements
So as
To thwart the achievable.

The Taking of Life

He who cannot give life
Should abstain from taking it,
Otherwise,
In the act of taking,
He may consume his own.

Time

We should all abide
Our time
Even as time
Abides for us.

Understanding

More takes place outside
Of our understanding
Than does so
Within our understanding.

View of the Mind

Memories seem to be the
Receptacle of summation.
Visions seem to be the
Vehicle of transformation.

Viewpoint

God is blamed
And credited by man
For more things
Than He is deserving.

Section B
Select Poems

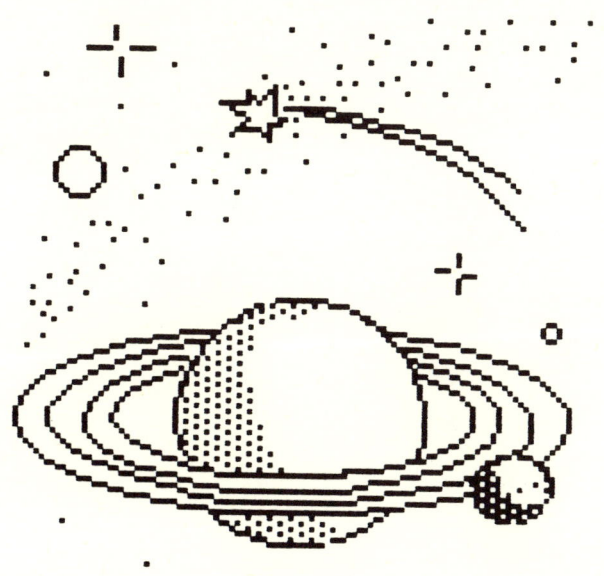

Introductory Remarks

In my first published volume, *Poetic Perceptions* (New York: Vantage Press, 1991), the book's entirety was composed of a variety of poems written at various times in my life. I could have included many other poems but chose instead to limit their number.

Here in this section, "Select Poems," I once again have offered some of my poetry for perusal. In this instance, I have only presented a few so as not to compete with the other sections, "Gems of Wisdom," and "Select Essays." Only those poems that I feel complement the scope and character of *Read My Mind* are included.

I hope you find my selections worthy.

All throughout My Life

All throughout my life
I searched to find identity,
Some clue I knew would certainly
Reveal whence, where, I came.

All throughout my life
My father was the cutting edge.
Desertion was his driving wedge
To more than just his wife.

Think about the suffering
All his progeny would bear.
You know they'd cry and miss him.
"Daddy's gone . . . to who knows where!"

I seem to be the only one
To seek and search and ask.
Oh no, I've never faltered
From this sad and lonely task.

All throughout my life
This vigil has been haunting me.
The person who I might have been
Stands saddened and lame.

Dear God

I'm so grateful to you.
You have given me life.
You have afforded me time to learn,
to understand, and to love.
You have provided me additional measures
of experience in which to grow.
You've allowed me a time to reap
and a time to sow.
In your care I have found new friendships
and mended many a broken fence.
I have challenged the future.
I have considered the past.
And along the way
I have watched my children and grandchildren
come of age.
Few moments have been free of pain.
Fewer still have I displayed despair.
For I have not lost the will to listen,
nor the ability to speak my voice.
My bounty is fruitful.
Through my loved ones and you
my harvest has been very, very rich.
From the bottom of my soul . . . I thank you!

How I See It

We've all had happy times. We've all had sad.
We store our memories, some good, some bad.

We've dreamed of being rich while being poor.
We've had our piece of cake and craved some more.

We've had our ups and downs, sometimes a fling.
Who hasn't lost a round or felt some sting?

But while we talk of life or simply dream,
The simple truth no doubt—remains supreme.

We've seen the world at war, sometimes at peace.
We've heard new life begin and watched it cease.

We're sending men in space. They study ways
To help the lives of man in future days.

Our science marches on at quickened pace.
Yet few can comprehend this frenzied race.

But while we seek new worlds and speculate,
The answers we want most have got to wait.

How's Your Mileage?

You say your car gets twenty-five miles per gallon!
You say you got a good bargain at the store!
This is great.
This is fine.
But tell me about your being.
What sort of bargain has it been?
Are you getting good mileage from yourself?
Are you happy with the good you've accomplished?
Are you at peace within?
Have you given as much as you've been given?
Have you helped as much as being helped?
Are there debts you've left unpaid
or friendships you never made?
Do you feel for those around you?
Do you offer aid when none is asked?
Maybe you're too quick to condemn.
Maybe you see less than the blind.
Maybe you hear what you want to hear.
Maybe, just maybe,
you think too much of you
and too little of the other guy.
Now why not get up tomorrow morning
and ask yourself:
"Would this world be a better place
if I got better mileage from myself?"

Man Is Not Almighty

Man cannot think he is almighty
when the lowly alleycat can see things he doesn't;
when spiders of every description can weave
webs of strength beyond his own ability;
where insects of uncountable shapes or varieties
hold secrets he can only dream about.
Even fish in the ocean,
fowl in the air, possess
navigational and homing perceptions of superiority.
Life, wherever it is found,
or in whatever form it has been conceived,
holds some measure of dominance.
Man's own progress is replete with examples
of copying life to sustain his own accomplishments.
No, *man is not almighty*!
Like the life he surveys,
he is but a variety.
He is buoyed by the promise of his dominion.
But he is not almighty.
His words,
his deeds,
his pursuits
should ever echo that acknowledgment;
otherwise he may deceive himself profoundly.

Reflection

Reflection is good for the soul.
It is like a fine dinner,
soothing, warming, and nutritional.
The many virtues we derive
can be compared with vitamins and minerals.
Reflection is man's telephone of sorts.
Thoughts are like utterings,
examination like consideration.
We are in tune with ourselves
instead of a voice on the line.
We are that voice.
We do the bemusing.
We are the providers of information.
And that quiet period within ourselves
opens channels and pathways
to our ultimate understanding.
Don't hang up!
Don't avoid such glorious moments!
Thankfully, they are plugged into our destiny.

What Is Time?

Think of time as the sea.
Think of time as the sand in an hourglass.
Think of time as flowing on air.
Think of time as parts of your hand.
Think of it as me.
Think of it as grand.
Think of it as debonair.
Think of it as moments on hand.
No event can be joined without it.
No happening can be measured without it.
No timetable exists but for it.
People both love and abhor it.
Time is all things.
Time is encompassing.
Time is all-fulfilling.
Time is always there.
Sometimes, it is not sufficient.
Sometimes, it is too abundant.
Sometimes, it is our enemy.
Sometimes, it is our friend.
Is its identity so difficult to see?
Is it an apex or apogee?
Maybe, we and time are the same.
Maybe, our egos are what is to blame.
Time is a place.
Time is a thing.
Time is unreal
yet still comes full-swing!

Who Is Perfect?

The earth is not a perfect place.
Man himself is not perfect.
No science,
no doctrine,
no code of ethics,
no religion,
and no professed way of conduct on earth is perfect.
Only God is perfect.
In Him we must place our trust.
It is He that leads us above our failings.
It is He who can deliver us to salvation.
Salvation itself implies freedom from wrong or
wrongdoings.
Physicality is a bastard to spirituality.
It is not possible to substitute one for the other.
Understanding that man is not perfect,
understanding that the earth, like man, is physical,
we have to conclude that Spirit is above both.
In dealing with the complexities of this seeming
unanswerable thought,
we must become aware that mere whispers,
mere urges from our being,
are but the start of a joyous venture.
The vision of lofty goals coupled with the venture itself
is a pathway to God and the Almighty.

Section C
Select Essays

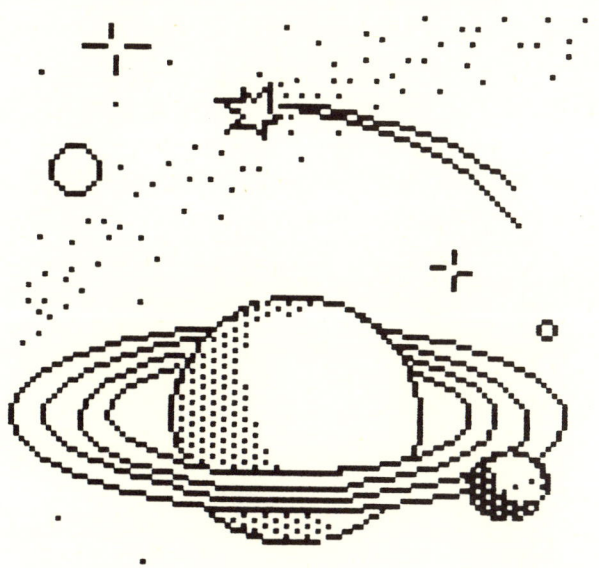

Introductory Remarks

When I was a boy, I have to admit that I was a diary freak. I kept simple notations about what excited me—girls, secret codes, parental problems, etc. Five-and-dime diaries seldom had much room for amplification on any subject. Therefore, later on I went to a stationery store and purchased a hardbound, lined journal, so I could write to my heart's content.

Once I was out of high school and into the military, my administrative job provided more opportunity to type my infrequent entries. Thus began what I called "Thoughts for the Day." These were actually essays written about some subject matter pertaining to either my activities or my insights.

All the original diaries, journals, and typewritten material from grade school through my military experience were lost, due to one reason or another—generally my frequent moves.

Around the beginning of the 1960s, I resumed these infrequent "excursions" of the mind with the previous title, "Thoughts for the Day," saving them in folders and three-ring binders. Once again, many were lost because of neglect. But throughout the 1970s I took better care of my ongoing writing efforts.

Early in the 1980s, I decided to work on those that had survived and submitted a collection of them to various book publishers. Following a dozen or more "rejection slips," two options seemed open to me: 1) publish them myself or 2) obtain a literary agent to secure a publisher for my book. I chose the latter.

I contacted a well-known New York agent and paid his fee of $300 in advance to review my manuscript of over one hundred essays. Several weeks later, I received his ten-page critique. Naturally, it commended me in most areas and criticized me in others. The climax to all this was, as he put it, "The public isn't interested in other people's thoughts. Even noted persons have great difficulty in being published. Commercially, it would be a dud. I suggest you put your talent to work on something more commercially oriented. Read what is on the best-seller list."

In 1986, Robert Fulgrum's book, *All I Really Need to Know I Learned in Kindergarten,* was published. To date, this book of "uncommon thoughts on common things" has sold over 4 million copies. So much for the literary agent's advice and expertise!

In this section of *Read My Mind,* I have selected twenty-three essays to present. The choices were not easy. I sincerely believe the substance and variety are commensurate with the scope of this book.

A Look Skyward

(November 29, 1988)

I looked at the heavens tonight from my blackened and secluded courtyard. There, to the east at about ten o'clock high, was the constellation of Orion, surrounded by many other stars, none of which I could identify.

It's such a clear evening, I thought to myself. *I wonder how many stars I could count in the small area I view?* Thus I began. By the time I gave up, the number was somewhere between seventy and eighty, a sizable figure for such an infinitesimal portion of the universe itself. Later, as I headed back into the house, I was taken back by the gigantic comparison that filtered into my mind.

Our planet Earth lies in the "Milky Way." Within this galaxy are millions of stars, of which our very sun is but one of those stars. The measurable universe is made up of billions of galaxies. My count of seventy to eighty stars was so small in comparison. What did it tell me?

It led me to realize that our eyes, in seeing, see only a portion, a very, very small fraction, of all there is to see. Since the eyes are only one of our body's sensing tools, are the other senses limited in similar proportions? If such is the case, we humans are in some respect virtually blind to a greater reality.

Presently our scientific prowess has furnished us with other means of surveying. Infrared and radar are two examples of this prowess. Such instruments are designed to give the exact information man is seeking and could thus be considered a prejudicial calibration. This is not to say they're not of value. It is to state instruments seek and do what they were designed to do. Telephones, for example, are marvelous instruments by which we communicate with one another by voice. They cannot measure gas or reveal any components of the real world. Thus they are prejudiced. By this comparison, you're more aware there are a greater number of things telephones cannot do than, in fact, they do.

Other examples from our world and our technological marvels only make it more apparent we see far less than is present, understand far less than is yet to be understood. None of us should be so blinded by our achievements as to thwart the achievable.

My experience this evening proved I could see only a fraction of what was present in the area I viewed. The road to complete, comprehensible intelligence and awareness is equally obscured, and all that is present has to be far greater than any of us previously imagined. I would suggest it is as infinite as the heavens we survey in a look skyward.

A Lucky Man

(January 19, 1978)

I am truly a lucky man!

I have a lovely, faithful wife, who is full both of wit and warmth; a comfortable home that is neither ostentatious nor beneath our means. I have three grown children, all of whom are separated from me both by miles and diversity in their manner of living, but who have gifted us at this writing with six precious grandchildren.

I feel honored in that I have two mothers who are both alive, alert, and able to function for themselves. Both are full of love and empathy. Each one finds, however, a different means of expressing her love. One a rose, one a daffodil, both beautiful and both different.

I am also lucky in that I have been granted new life in recent years in which to pursue my interests, having been rescued from the bowels of death by modern medical achievements. In this light, I have accepted my condition graciously, exhibiting the tenacity to live as a normal human being. Not hiding from work, but rather instead I have sought new goals, embarked on physical tasks and projects I would not have attempted in healthier days.

Whether by blind innocence, uncommon maturity, or stubborn convictions, I approach each day with a sense of faith—faith in a power greater than I am (but yet vested in me), that what will be, will be! *Destiny* is a single word to explain this. Belief in the Almighty is another. But

83

whatever your religious persuasion, the fact remains: I have joy in my life, happiness in my waking hours, and great self-satisfaction in my accomplishments.

With all of this, I have been rewarded an abundance of friends with whom to share this good fortune.

This truly makes me a lucky man!

A Pause to Refresh

(April 26, 1981)

Dawn is breaking at the moment. A low cloud cover has pushed inland from the ocean lying to my west. A very fine mist permeates the air outside. Sparrows, for miles around, are twittering, singing, and flying from tree to tree. Their voices, in a harmonic crescendo, sound like an army of cicadas. Against this background I can hear the territorial calls of different mockingbirds in the neighborhood chasing some intruder, and occasionally I hear their magnificent variety of songs.

Down the street, a car door closes and a grinding starter momentarily pierces this symphony of dawn. This is followed by short bursts of revving the engine, then a gradual drone of shifting gears coming closer and closer. Varoooooom, it goes past our house, wet tires smacking at the asphalt roadbed.

As it subsides beyond my range of hearing, a languid stillness is interrupted only by creaks and groans of timber, plaster, and paint, as various joints in the foundation of our home expand and contract from the sun's rays now breaking through, sending warmth toward earth.

Silence again. It is still everywhere. Now I can hear a cadence. Ta-boom, ta-boom, ta-boom—my own heart ticking an incessant parody of some clock. The momentary silence ends, and everywhere life is tuning up like an orchestra before the concert begins.

Listening to the world around me is a wonderful, exhilarating experience. Man needs to do this from time to time. Too often his preoccupation with himself brings about a lack of symmetry with nature. Man forgets he is part of nature itself, certainly not its master. Here, he frequently finds the real and unreal reversed, because he has reversed them. I suppose this accounts for the many dilemmas and dogmas associated with comprehension of the simple and complex sides of nature. By man's inability to equate his life with nature, the nature of life cannot be equated. The secret of simplicity is masked. Worlds within worlds and life beyond life are just a jumble of words. Peripheral vision and perception are weak.

Man believes what he wants to believe. He hears what he wants to hear. His senses are dulled by his own admission into a shell of submission.

Life is a learning experience. Love is a teaching experience. The two combined bring about a spiritual experience. We may all bide our time, as even time abides for us. It is well that periodically we take a moment to pause and refresh our psyches.

Dear Mrs. Ford

(March 21, 1988)

Fifty years ago, as a small boy, I dressed in my very best clothes and trudged off to Sunday school each week. I daresay most boys who have gone to Sunday school had their reservations about what to expect. I did. But I liked every bit of it, especially the singing.

My church, Olivet Presbyterian Church, in Prospect Park, Pennsylvania, was a beautiful stone structure with generous amounts of stained-glass windows on three sides, reflecting biblical stories in their scenes. Sunday school was held in the basement. Very rarely could one find an empty seat. It was so well attended by children and adults alike.

Quite by accident one Sunday morning, as I turned around to look at the people seated behind me, I caught the eyes of a little old lady several rows back. I smiled at her. She seemed quite pleased. On subsequent weeks, when I looked back at the crowd, this sweet old lady had her eyes fixed upon me. I smiled at her, and she radiated with delight.

It was always the same from Sunday to Sunday. At some point in time, I learned this lady was the mother of one of the Sunday school teachers. In fact, her daughter later became my own teacher. One week, she took me aside from the other children in the class and said, "Jerry, my mother is just ecstatic when you turn around and smile at her." I found that difficult to understand. But I felt warmed by the compliment.

As the weeks passed, my Sunday school teacher became one of my very best childhood friends. She took my brother, Michael, and me on hikes, outings, and even to the Maryland country farm where she had relatives. She would always send me home with "goodies" and made sure tears in my clothes were repaired. She saved me from many a whipping and punishment by so doing.

Soon I was a regular visitor to their old Victorian three-story house. It was spellbinding. It had sleeping porches on the upper floors, an attic, a basement, and an endless number of solid doors separating rooms. You couldn't go from one room to another without a heavy hand-carved door to open and close. In my childish imagination, there were all kinds of secret passageways somewhere off the front and back staircases. Every place in the house was an adventure of sorts.

One Sunday afternoon, in the kitchen, I helped clean some of the vegetables for Mrs. Ford while she was preparing a splendid dinner. Her heavy cast-iron stove was fired from wood instead of the customary gas or electric we know today. It was magnificent. The smell and the taste of food prepared in that stove were above anything I remember in my life.

She inquired about my family, my foster parents, brothers and sisters. I told her what I knew. Much of what I related disturbed her. During one of those conversations, she confided in me. "Jerry," she said, "I don't know what I would do if you weren't there in Sunday school come Sundays. I look forward so much to seeing you turn around and smile at me." My childish mind could not fathom what all of that meant. To me, I did nothing out of the ordinary. And I told her so. She continued, however, by saying, "Do you know Jerry, I think I come to Sunday school as much to see you greet me with your smile as for any other reason?"

I can't remember how I answered her. Most likely I blushed, for I blushed a lot in those days. "But," she went on, "you see, Jerry, very few people smile at me. Rarely, if ever, a child. They look at me as an old lady. They often turn their heads to avoid looking at me entirely. I watch your every move. And when you turn around to look for me, then smile, it makes me feel good all over. Can you understand that?" I said I did in the same polite, sincere manner she had spoken to me.

Later, as an adult, and captivated by my present wife, Penny, I learned more of what that smile represented. Of all the many beautiful features about Penny, it was her smile that touched me inside. So much, in fact, I wrote a song about it called "A Smile." The professional arranger whom I commissioned to score the music and lyrics suggested I change the title of my song. "Nobody will care for a song called 'A Smile,'" he said. "Call it 'Penny.' Everyone likes a song that has a woman's name." I accepted his advice as practical and professional. After all, he had been in the music business many years.

Some months later, the most popular song in our country was "The Shadow of Your Smile." I laughed to myself, recalling the professional's proclamation that "nobody will care for a song about a smile."

The memory of dear Mrs. Ford remains with me still. Because of her, I can honestly tell myself how important is the simple act of a smile. I also realize that she made a greater impact upon me (it would appear) than her daughter—my Sunday school teacher—whose name I have long forgotten.

Destiny Drives Us

(April 16, 1988)

Life is multifaceted. I'm sure you recognize this fact. Most of the facts remain hidden, however. A good example would be observing rays of the sun penetrating your room on a cold, clear day. You only see one color, but by placing a prism to catch the sunlight passing through it, you see a spectrum of many colors. I'm sure our life is faceted similarly.

A former buddy of mine in the air force, Joseph Steppart, was a lifelong philosopher. He is responsible for my philosophical outlook today. By my association with him, my world opened up and was altered for all time. Few of my beliefs cannot be traced back to his guidance and friendship. Our solitary discussions were lessons destined for the future. I have tried, unsuccessfully, to locate him in recent years.

Frequently I am reminded of the seeds sown in our discussions years ago. They have borne fruit beyond my expectations. Even today, newer branches are reaching out for newer understanding.

My work today was centered in our music room. I wrote interpretations for many of my musical compositions. I could reflect upon a reality that, up to now, had escaped me. Because of Joe Steppart, I became a firm believer in destiny. Quite often I lose contact with it. I think I try to control it. Possibly, I think I am master of it.

90

But today I recognized we are only passengers of our destiny—rather than the pilots or captains of ships. Much of what we do (being preordained) fits a picture—a picture we are part of, rather than being the picture itself. How could I explain that to you in more explicit terms? Well, maybe by explaining how I came to understand it or accept it.

Throughout the last twenty-five years, a large variety of creative activity has occupied my world. It is like a cornucopia. Little prearrangement seems to have been at my own authority. I merely reacted to some inner dictate.

As time has passed, and without a recognizable blueprint, pieces or fragments of all this work have cemented together in a more complete tapestry.

Winston Churchill was quoted as saying, "This is the end of the beginning or the beginning of the end." That is ever so appropriate here. At no point in the twenty-five years of working with my music, poetry, essays, etc., could I say precisely where I was—beginning of the end or end of the beginning. There seemed little doubt. There wasn't even any semblance of order.

Suddenly, like a puzzle, glimpses of a picture began to emerge. I worked harder. I got frustrated. I got angry. I even swore I was trying to insert pieces that didn't fit, and thus no finished picture emerged.

I have come to face a new reality. I must follow my instincts and forget about seeing either an end or a beginning. We can set goals for accomplishments. But do we ever accomplish our goals? We only contribute to a greater goal and a greater accomplishment. We are learning by experience. We are fulfilling a destiny. Destiny drives us. Following the dictates of our destiny, we are moving to a place in time, in space, and in unison with preordained orders.

Like the flow of blood or the movement of tars, we are riding the tide of an energy force. Perhaps you'd like to think of the force as a command. We are doing precisely what we were designed to do. We all have a design, genetic or otherwise, to fulfill a purpose. I can assure you we are fulfilling it.

I look back amazed at all the various directions I seem to have traveled in my life. They seemed a bit disjointed. This evening I see very clearly the opposite is the truth. All I have done has been patterned to a given end. I am almost breathless to continue my work. There is much to be done. Physical impairments tell me time is short, and physical reasoning in a physical world is not often wrong.

I am giddy. I am happy. I am anxious to pursue any and all of my creative ideas. They are the anointment of my destiny.

Do I Want to Live?

(December 2, 1987)

Although I don't remember, it must have coursed through my mind the morning of November 24, 1972, when I had the telltale pains of angina in my chest and the radiating heat accompanying them. My arms felt as though I had been lifting too many weights.

I went to work, however, suspecting all was not right. These symptoms, matching those I had read about, gave me some concern, to be sure. At that point, I must have said to myself, "Do I want to live?"

I had my secretary, Delores, call for an ambulance. "Get an ambulance here. I think I am having a heart attack." Before it arrived, I had been stricken by a massive coronary and slumped from my place at the desk, backward, against the wall, and onto the floor. In more classic terms, I had a "myocardial infarction." My heart had stopped beating. My color turned blue. There was no breathing. There was no sign of life.

Fortunate for me on that morning, my warehouseman, Dennis Taylor, summoned to the office by Delores DiNino, had just completed a course in CPR: cardiopulmonary resuscitation. He began administering to me immediately before the ambulance arrived.

It was a total blackout for me, except as I was gaining consciousness from Dennis's help. I saw a dear elderly friend of mine—Hugh "Scotty" Stewart—displayed in his military uniform as sergeant with the American flag hanging on the wall behind him.

"Relax your hands, Jerry," I heard a voice telling me. It was Dennis. To me, my hands were relaxed. In glancing at them, I saw they were stiff and clenched as if I were still grasping for the desk I had fallen from earlier.

The ambulance had not arrived yet. It was only Dennis and Delores attending me. At that moment, the same question must have coursed through my mind. *Do I want to live?*

One of my salesmen, Frank DeNino, came into the warehouse. I asked if he would go to the nearby drugstore and get some nitroglycerin tablets. That action revealed I was in command of my mental faculties. I was certainly telling myself I wanted to live. He quickly returned and I put one of the small white tablets under my tongue. Soon after, the ambulance arrived. It had been held up in a traffic accident on the freeway.

I was transported to the Riverside Community Hospital, where I remained on the critical list for twenty-eight days. My blood pressure during the first few days was indiscernible. During that month's sojourn, I must have subconsciously asked myself over and over again, *Do I want to live?* I say that because each time the nurses took my blood pressure they would comment, "I don't know what is keeping you alive; you've got no blood pressure."

Thus began the chain of hospitalizations that have become so numerous that I can't keep track of them anymore. First it was in Denver, Colorado, following a trial return to working in my business. I was there attending a convention of professional photographers and wound up in the hospital suffering some arterial closure. The feelings, then as now, have always been the same: Inside my body there is a sudden uneasiness. Something isn't right.

Like a minor earthquake, there is a sudden jolt in the body, with temporary visual impairment. In quick succession there is radiating heat across the chest. Functional behavior becomes more and more difficult. Breathing does not seem to produce oxygen into the lungs. There is an unconscious response of the body to tense. Anxiety begins and is soon followed by mental fear. Although a bona fide heart attack may or may not be taking place, the calamity of events is real. A crisis is in progress, and medical help is required immediately.

The symptoms that day proceeded to incapacitate me. I was rushed to Denver General Hospital. Once on oxygen, along with an IV delivering lidocaine into the heart, I soon recovered enough for the trauma team to dismiss me with ten milligrams of Valium and instructions to get out of the high altitude and return to California as soon as possible.

As I look back upon that specific chain of events, I marvel that I was able to make it home alone. In truth, I was a very, very sick man on the brink of death once more. Inside, some unconscious query must have prodded me on: *Do I want to live?* Only a couple of months later, I was given quadruple bypass surgery at the Loma Linda University Medical Center, in Loma Linda, California, to save my life. Two of my major coronary arteries were 100 percent closed. Another was occluded 90 percent, which meant I was literally living on a trickle of blood. It explained why I would pass out even by talking with someone.

Coronary bypass surgery was in its infancy at the time. My own doctor was among those who disapproved of the controversial procedure. Through my own determination, my own decision, I sought help from those practitioners who were using it for heart patients.

Through the years, my heart has stopped beating on more than one occasion. The first was my massive coronary itself. The second instance was the deliberate stopping of the heart during the bypass surgery. My heart stopped again during surgery for removal of my gallbladder in 1977. I was "defibrillated" on the operating table, and the surgery continued. And it has seemed to stop beating at other times, but which I learned was a long pause before an erratic heartbeat. That is very frightful as is "arrhythmia," where the heart goes into wild, seemingly uncontrollable beating. I remember one humorous instance concerning this arrhythmia when I was in the intensive-care unit of Loma Linda UMC Hospital. Penny was visiting me at the time. Suddenly a team of doctors, interns, nurses, and God knows who else came rushing in. Seeing me in conversation with Penny and sitting up without any undue concern, one doctor asked if I felt alright.

"I feel fine," I responded.

And he in turn said, "Do you know what has just happened to you?"

"Sure, I know, and I already took care of that!"

It seems as though the monitors had revealed I was having an attack of arrhythmia, and this is a very unpredictable, frequently fatal situation. As the doctors continued interviewing and questioning me when I revealed I knew what had taken place, they said, "What do you mean by 'taking care of that'?"

Almost in a jovial response, but really quite serious, I explained. "I get these attacks quite often, and I have found the best way to deal with them is to take a deep breath, be calm, and then suddenly explode with the command, STOP THAT!" This jolted everyone. Some laughed. Some looked on in disbelief. While others seemed too dumbfounded to express any emotion. I was cautioned not to depend upon that method, and I was put on a medication to help control the problem: *Do I want to live?*

Following my original bypass surgery in 1973, the team of surgeons who attended me stated that, on the basis of their knowledge, I could expect to live another five years even considering the enormity of damage done to my heart. Put simply, the entire back of my heart was destroyed.

In 1976, while I was on an automobile trip to New York, two of the three bypasses closed. It happened just after I entered the Alamo in San Antonio, Texas. I spent a week at St. Mary's Hospital, while my wife, Penny, and her friend Jessie Merman took refuge in a local motel.

Upon release, we all continued to drive east. But I once again had to be rushed to Lankenau Hospital in Philadelphia, Pennsylvania, with yet another minor closure.

I seem to have become a regular patient at many hospitals, with basically the same sequence of events responsible for my admission. In 1987, tests at the VA Hospital at Loma Linda revealed that only 41 percent of my heart tissue was alive. In other words, 59 percent of my heart muscle was dead. The angiography done at that time showed that my only remaining artery was open, but it had five—count them: five—closures, or "stenoses," along its pathway. Surgeons agreed that in my case, no surgical intervention was possible to improve my condition.

I sought to have my personal cardiologist at Loma Linda UMC give me his approval to become a heart transplant patient. It was his considered opinion that I could not enjoy the quality of life I already possessed with a risky heart transplant. He went on to explain all of the options. I was disappointed and sought to have the surgery done elsewhere, but all of the facilities I approached concurred in his opinion.

As from the very beginning of my battle with heart disease, it has been my awareness of my own body, my own openness with doctors, and my own intelligence that have served me as tools to survive. Some I act upon. Some I do not. Some of my reasons for doing what I do in the course of a given day are valid. Others, as you might suspect, are not.

Although we all would like to believe we are masters of our own destiny, circumstantial evidence is sufficient to imply this is more often just wishful thinking. I am of the opinion, however, that the mind is very powerful and can accomplish miracles. Lacking such power, the physical body, like my ninety-two-year-old friend, Joe Friedenthal, has stated, "does not wish to die."

With my longevity in doubt, I seem to persist from day to day with a statement under my breath: "Do I want to live?"

Note

As of January 19, 1992, as this manuscript was being readied for mailing to the publisher, the amount of live tissue in my heart had shrunk to 23 percent.

Eternal Order of Things

(October 19, 1974)

If I were asked to define a part of man's place in the eternal order of things, I would begin by stating: Look ahead to the future. Take account of all the things you see in the present. Reexamine the events of the past. For in so doing, you'll discover, as would any keen observer, tomorrow is a cacophilios* repetition of yesterdays, of moments lived and relived.

In it, you'll find the same love, as well as the same heartaches, the same innocence and idealism of youth, the same sweetness and selfishness of a babe. New experiences are merely a redress of older ones. You'll see the world turbulent, seething in an endless parade of sanctity and sin, as it has been from its very creation. There can be neither total peace nor total war. For if earth had one without the other, it would cease to exist. Its duality is the umbilical cord and the salvation of all that is cherished in our daily intercourse. It provides us our sustenance for the discernible future.

All things that have been will be again, in different

Cacophilios is my own coined word implying the duality of nature in man: love versus hate, good opposing bad. It is from the Greek *kakos* (bad) and *philos* (love). I added the letter *i* to *philos,* making it *philios* to intersperse the singular ego—"I."

guises perhaps. But as cycles, rebirth, renewal of spirit, and reincarnation laws dictate, the keys to the future are bound by our past. Man, as such, is bound by his mistakes, guided by his deeds, elevated by his sacrifice, and, most important, redeemed by his love.

In this light, he is a creature ever-changing as the weather, mimicking things seen and unseen. He is a traveler in space, but an inhabitant of the earth. Where earth goes, he goes. However earth fares, so also is the prescription for man. Plotting earth's destiny is no doubt one of man's subliminal and subconscious pursuits. Seemingly all his actions can be answered by this supposition: "Comprehending earth's relationship with our defined universe is most likely our ultimate goal. Pursuing that destiny is surely our most lofty ambition." In and of itself, that is man's place in the eternal tapestry.

Give It Up

(August 17, 1974)

I've often been confronted by people in my life with the statement: "Give it up!" or, "Why don't you give it up!" Both exclamatory remarks are frequently issued in a tone of forcefulness.

All too frequently, these same well-meaning individuals follow their own advice, taking the easy road, the more comfortable byways. Their reasoning is simple: if you have to labor too long, it's too much trouble. And they are usually the very same people who suggest if you can't go in through the front door, try the back. If the back is locked, break a window.

This is how they reckon with life, with work, and no doubt with love. Most certainly, it applies to things calling for patience and dedication or pursuit with a purpose. They don't bother! Because they don't bother, you shouldn't bother. What is okay for them is okay for you. Because they have no trouble, you shouldn't have any trouble.

The trouble with that brand of philosophy is that it fosters a reliance on conditioned comforts. By suggesting you give it up, they feel you shouldn't be doing it in the first place. They think perhaps someone will do it for you. Or they really don't want you to do it because they can't or probably wouldn't think of doing it for themselves.

The latter of those three probabilities, to wit, they

don't want you to do it, is most likely the hidden truth of the matter.

People are envious of determination. They are leery of motivation. But they are all too often downright jealous of inspiration. Thus they avoid and suggest you avoid perspiration. "Give it up!" they say.

Are they thinking of your health? Are they offering to take over your role? Your job? Maybe they legitimately feel you'd do better to put your talents to some other use. It's possible. It's feasible. It sounds good. But frankly, this is very, very unlikely. They really want you to be their equal, not their superior, even their pawn—and thus their inferior. That's what they want. And it becomes possible with the use of such phrases: "Give it up!" "Where is that going to get you?" "Don't work so hard." "Why are you wasting your time on that?"

I'm reminded of an incident in my life some years ago when I was a young salesman. I was very dedicated, using all of my skills of persuasion, charm of conversation, and administrative aptitudes routinely. For me, at the time, I was going someplace. The home office would frequently send out communications to various offices in the country of how great a job I was doing, to influence other salesmen. I'd even get personal calls from various regional supervisors complimenting me on my performance.

One day, my boss, from San Francisco, took me out to dinner. Following a scrumptious meal, he got my attention. "Jerry," he said, "give it up." I was suddenly very ill at ease, wondering if I had done something against the company rules. I couldn't imagine what he had in mind.

"What do you mean by that?" I asked.

"You've got a lot to learn," he told me as he went on. "Who's your boss?" The question was gruff, but he had a smile on his face that belied his real intent.

Without any hesitation on my part, I said he was.

"Well," he started out. "I expect to remain your boss for some time to come!"

This was the prelude to a rather lengthy discourse on some of life's realities. I was commanding a considerable amount of attention from the home office by my efforts. They berated him for not getting all the other salesmen to follow my lead. Perhaps there were still other things he didn't mention. The point here is that by such a determined effort on my part, I was becoming a threat to his job. "Give it up!" he said. "Give it up!"

My choice was very simple. I didn't give it up. In fact, I pursued my job as always—maybe subconsciously with more fervor than before. And that choice taught me a lesson in life.

A month or so after, he saw to it that I was ousted from not only the position I held, but from the company itself. It was a bitter pill. In time, I recovered from that shock and moved on to better things in my life.

If, like me, you believe in yourself (or want to), be wary of those presumed well-intentioned people who say to you, "Give it up!" Life may have its freeways scattered about, but they had to be built. They had to be envisioned, planned, and blueprinted, all before a single drop of concrete was laid.

Listen to your desires. Cling to your drives. Enjoy the dreams you fashion. They are the mold from which much of the world was created. And they are the mark of an achiever. All these things are the traffic signals of one's destiny. It is far better to reach than not reach at all. It is far more gratifying to get up when you've been knocked down.

Life isn't the easy road. In reality, life is the hard road. Show me a successful person, and I'll show you someone who has strived to produce, labored to improve himself, and worked beyond the minute hands on the clock. At the same time, many a successful person who at this moment may sit in complacency would eagerly trade that soft chair for a chance to do it all over again. To be sure, it would be most difficult to find one successful person who has been convinced or persuaded to change his direction by someone telling him, "Give it up!"

God Bless

(January 1, 1976)

During one's lifetime there are many things upon which to reflect. There are those things we were always waiting to grow into as we aged and an equal number of things we hoped we would outgrow. Most of us, though no longer children, still find ourselves growing into or out of a plethora of situations.

As a child, I was anxious for my older brothers to outgrow their clothes so they could be passed on to me. That was an exciting anticipation. Although many of us see families buying new items for most of their children today, I'm sure there are large numbers of families to which the necessity of passing down clothes is financially sound and still practiced.

So many reminiscences similar to the above come to mind when I have time to reflect back. Some I like to recall. Others, more painful, I'd just as soon forget.

Kneeling beside the bed at night and saying prayers was something taught to me very early on. In the beginning, there were the simple prayers such as: "Now I lay me down to sleep, I pray the Lord my soul to keep." Such simplistic prayers were later replaced by the ever-familiar "Lord's Prayer" most Christians know by heart.

I had many different prayers of my own through the years. Usually, they were an addition at the end of reciting the Lord's Prayer. It was not uncommon for many of them to begin with the phrase, "God bless." It was God bless this person or that person who was sick, traveling to a distant place, starving, perhaps without the benefit of home and family. God bless my teachers. God bless those who did nice things for me. I always had a multitude of recipients for those gentle requests.

The nature and content of prayers change in our lives, as indeed we change. As I have already noted, there are the prayers of a child. There are the prayers of a confused adolescent or the fervent awakening of faith in some young adult. Prayers from adults are usually filled with more personal requests. And as they mature, the children and grandchildren become more often those needing God's attention.

When my busy days are over, I retire to the bedroom exhausted. Truly I am ready to lie down and go to sleep. I admit I have become lazy. Rarely do I kneel beside the bed to say my prayers. I meditate quietly within myself, beseeching God to mold me into a better person. I ask Him to help me understand those things that confound me. I give thanks for the fact I enjoyed another day of life. I also confide many things in Him about myself, not as one would expect in a confessional, but more as an open discussion. And I ask forgiveness for any things I believe warrant forgiveness.

Most always the last words I utter of any prayer, whether it be aloud or in silence, are: "God bless the man who invented the bed." The bed is a wonderful place of refuge and renewal of energy for a tired body. I cannot go to sleep comfortably until I have made known my appreciation.

Letter to Mr. Minnick

(March 12, 1985)

Dear Mr. Minnick:

When bedtime came for me as a small boy and I put my head to the foot of the bed to catch whatever air was stirring outside, I could peer through the rusty, corroding screens of my upstairs bedroom and see you with your back to me. Your aged wife, usually in her long nightgown, rocked back and forth in a most beautiful oak rocker, seemingly in a trance.

You didn't know then I was a silent observer to the scene unfolding. I didn't feel as though I was a Peeping Tom, nor an intruder. I was simply a small boy with my eyes and ears captivated by the scene.

You sat at your piano playing and singing a whole array of lilting Irish music and songs. "Danny Boy" seemed to be your opening selection each night. And if my memory serves me right, "When Irish Eyes Are Smiling" was frequently the finale. I especially liked "In the Gloaming," because it typified those hot, humid, and sultry nights when everyone had all their windows wide open for some relief.

I suppose at the beginning it was curiosity more than anything else that was apparent in my little world. How funny it was to see an old man, crippled with arthritis and bent by age, sit down at the piano each night to sing for a decrepit, equally old woman.

The notes floated on the summer air, accompanied by the feeble humming of your missus. Hordes of crickets, both near and far, seemed to provide the perfect orchestral vibrato to this melancholy concert. In due time, it lulled me to sleep, graced my dreams, and even more than that, it brought me to the window even when it wasn't hot or sticky. A seed of sorts had been planted—unknown to you, unknown to me. Words I wrote in one of my earliest musical compositions sublimely express that truth:

> Lost in the shadow of a past
> Forgotten long ago,
> Love as a seed was planted there
> And left to branch and grow!

Indeed, a seed was planted. The seed to which I am referring is music. But, in fact, music may only have been the outer shell, whereas the inner pulp—the meat, the fertile, life-giving care and sustenance—was love.

It took me all of fifty years to recognize that simple truth. Fifty years of intermittent desire, travels around the country, plus a variety of work and life-styles, before I was smart enough to comprehend the effect your humble piano playing had on my life. Pity that you were never to know of your good effect on a small child.

I am very grateful that, with maturity, I have learned some lessons about life. I want you to know that I value all you did for me, even if it was unconscious on your part. I treasure the melodic wisps of your influence in many of my musical compositions. Surely you even played a major role in my desire to play the piano and teach myself to compose. There are ever so many of my works that bear your signature in them and your personality. None is more charming and eloquent than the selection I composed titled "Pleasant Valley."

Bless you, Mr. Minnick, wherever you are.

Little Heart

(September 16, 1989)

Bolinas, California, is a very small town on the Northern California coast, hidden from much of the world by virtue of its inhabitants, who consistently remove all road signs or billboards that could betray its presence to tourists. My wife and I visited our children and grandchildren there earlier in the month while on a vacation jaunt. It would seem the town has basically two types of people: the haves and the have-nots. Most exhibit the dress and attitudes of the flower children generation.

Penny's son, Mikel Pruitt, lives in an old mobile coach, nestled beneath a decaying apple orchard. To the coach he has added a lean-to workshop, a bedroom, and other minor conveniences.

During our week-long stay with Mikel, I would go out for a small walk each morning, savoring the clean air and the enjoyment of various indigenous growth uncommon to my own environment in Southern California. The dirt road leading down to his place from the main highway is littered with rocks, none of which was interesting. All seemed to be a dull, gray color of some variety of sandstone.

Tuesday, September 6, I spotted a very small stone lying amid a debris of dust and rocks. It appeared to have a jasper color—reddish brown. I leaned over to pick it up in my hands. To my shock and surprise, it bore the color of a natural heart and was shaped as such also. The odds against my finding such a stone had to be incalculable. I could not help being moved by the incident, and I said words to the effect: "Little stone so smooth and rare, how many years have you awaited there? Aeons maybe, for such a baby. How often have you cried for love? Or sought to escape the ground's hold? You are now in my hands, little heart. You'll go with me wherever I go. You'll be a reminder of my own frailness. For I know within, the good Lord has me in His hands. My fingers will caress you. My energy will address you, hopefully imparting the love the Creator gives to all His children. Together, we'll go forward, giving strength and commitment to each other from this chance rendezvous."

Having recently endured the difficult news of being too old for a heart transplant, as well as an annual pronouncement from cardiologists I should not expect to live another year, I took this incident as a meaningful happening. I had been presented a little heart.

Note

At some place and time in 1991, I lost this little heart, which I had carried with me constantly. I can only presume it happened while I was wearing my favorite fifty-cent sportshirt, which had a minor tear in the seam of the breast pocket.

Look Around

(April 5, 1988)

Sometimes I think to myself that most of what man needs to know in this world can be found merely by observing nature around him. But people in the big cities, the urban sprawl, and maybe even the country are too busily engaged in making a living to pay much attention to nature.

Yet it is in nature where all the issues confronting man can be observed, studied, and assimilated for propelling him to greater awareness and newer heights.

Each time I ventured outside of the house today, I took a solitary walk. I saw things happening. It was both clear and hot. Suddenly I could see smog pouring into Riverside, enveloping the city like "The Mist" in Stephen King's novel of the same name. Subtle changes were taking place. Most of them took place without man's fuss or notice.

Completely unrelated, birds of various species were in the process of gathering nesting material. I observed the blackbirds in particular. Surprising to me, in just a few cursory glances I learned something I never knew before. One blackbird, busy at the task of gathering material for a nest, picked up brown, dead strips of palm leaves and flew off to a green oak tree in my neighbor's yard. It sat at the apex of the tree and pecked away until it had stripped apart a green leaf. By unbelievable dexterity, it retained both the dead strips of palm leaves and the new, green oak leaves in its beak. It then flew off to its nest, high above Central Avenue in a huge palm tree.

In all the years of observing birds building nests, this was the first time I had ever seen a bird collecting fresh, green vegetation along with dead strips, too. What was the purpose? A layman like myself can only ponder. I'm sure, however, that an experienced bird-watcher would immediately provide the answer.

Fifteen or twenty minutes later, while I was taking a break from my office work, my wife arrived home in her 1985 Dodge Lancer. The sun, now dipping in the western sky, was at such an angle to reveal two spiderwebs stretched from the hood of the car to a nearby tree, some ten feet away. I studied the relationship. It baffled me. How was it possible that in the space of only a few minutes a spider or spiders had spun two webs between the car and the tree? It was incredible. A masterful engineering feat was completed without detection. Only the afternoon sunset brought it to my attention. Could we humans do the same in such a short period of time? With all of our technology, we cannot.

No doubt, similar displays from nature are waiting for someone to observe if he looks around. Perhaps many of nature's secrets lie just outside our homes, like the two I have mentioned here.

Man's Finite Nature

(February 19, 1979)

The hour is late. In the stillness of night a million and one sounds permeate the silence. Insects. Automobiles on a distant highway. Airplanes high in the heavens bound for some unknown destination. The night is a time for those who love to ponder. It almost seems to be a miraculous time with an unseen energy recharging and revitalizing our mental senses. Senses that may have been dulled by the cannonlike activity of the day.

Somehow, this darkness, this quiet, becomes ethereal. I would imagine night is the time we can travel vicariously throughout the heavens. For as I understand, the void of space outside our known atmosphere is black—just like the night confronting us.

Standing on earth, gazing upward, we can see with increased perception the millions of pinpoint lights. We ask ourselves, "How is it possible that each of those lights represents a body hundreds of times larger than the earth upon which we stand?" It is here man must fathom his finite nature against the infinite he surveys. Here ego must submit before the mirror of infinity. Paradoxically, by submission man is given the inspiration to pursue the sciences, grapple with the concepts of creation, and come full circle to reinflate his ego once more.

Our containment, our keen vision, and our understanding seem to imply something very profound. With the rising, falling, inflating and deflating, expanding and contracting, we have a meager glimpse into the cosmos. And what we see but do not comprehend initially is that the cosmos is breathing! We are all within a gigantic breathing apparatus. Here might be a part of the logic of our very life—being a small thing inside a bigger thing!

We can gaze and marvel at the seeming disarray from horizon to horizon, asking ourselves, "Is there order or disorder?" But a thought I once had seems more revealing. It suggested simplicity is cloaked in the complex. And because the complex seems ever so confounding, few dare to seek the simple. It is those who seek to expand man's finite nature.

Our Home

(December 17, 1977)

I like to think of our home as the product of our ambitions, the jackpot of our good fortune, and a vivid example of friends' assistance, family financial help, and neighborly encouragement. All have played a primary role in its acquisition. Without them, this would be more formally a house. And we, most likely, would be passersby to the scene.

I like to view our home as something very special. Special in the sense that my wife, Penny, and I, as its principal occupants, place little emphasis on pretense or ceremony, choosing instead to welcome strangers and friends, relatives and in-laws, with equal exuberance, equal tolerance, and above all equal love! This makes a house a home. This endows occupants and visitors alike with a sense of belonging. It encourages a freedom of expression. It elicits a warmth of being rarely found, but hungrily sought after.

I like to imagine our home as sort of a world church. Certainly our guest books bear signatures of widespread visitors welcomed to share our home irrespective of their divergent philosophical, political, and religious beliefs. Within the walls of our home, each person acknowledges his own faith, expresses his own beliefs—in discussion and practice—usually with mutual forbearance and tolerance of the others' views.

115

Our home is a sacred place where in solitude the soul can contemplate, seek, question, and mature to its own heights without proselytizing or fear of reprisal or persecution by the primary tenants. This is accomplished amid the chatter of voices, the clatter of routine, and just plain living. Worship here is a form of action, as indeed action is a form of worship. The end result is that one within himself is mentally and physically expressing a variety of religious calisthenics.

I am happy to note our home is a place of amusement and entertainment for all those that enter, whether young or old. The generation gap is nonexistent. And prejudice of race, color, or creed is not discernible. Only the beholder can rightly attest one way or another.

Above all else, I am most thankful that our home is both a heaven and haven for me, wherein each day offers solace, gains newly found purpose, encourages greater goals, and rewards us with satisfaction of our accomplishments, deeper appreciation of our fortune, sincerity of our associates, and richness of our love together.

This I am proud to call our home!

Prayer and Discussion

(March 21, 1989)

(The following is a prayer and discussion I had with my Lord while standing outside in my front yard earlier this evening.)

Lord, as I look to the heavens, my heart and soul are always with you. I treasure your works. I glory in how miraculous this earth is, albeit we men seem bent upon its destruction.

In talking with you, Lord, I recognize that the act itself is expressive of a great deal of faith. I say this because I have not consciously seen what most call a physical image of you. Yes, you are a part of the wind, the sky, the seeds in the ground, the grass upon which I stand, the birds that now nest for the night. The moon now rising is a part of you. I, who stand here so insignificant and small, am a part of you. There is little I can see or think of that is not a part of you. You are everything and everywhere, and for such a small creature as myself, it is a greatness almost too difficult to imagine and perceive, let alone picture in a physical image.

What do we know of you? Well, we know that you rule and command the universe. You are said to have created Adam and Eve, they being the first humans on this earth, from which all men were spawned. I know also of your coming to prove yourself and your heavenly father in

117

heaven. You were born in a little town called Bethlehem in Judea. You were taught by the Essenes. You did great things such as raising the dead, healing the sick, and performing all manner of miracles in your time. You gave so much of yourself that man hated you. You spoke truth where people only heard of lies and misconceptions. This frightened them. This terrorized them. So fearful were they that leaders of communities and nations were fearful of you. In the end, they tried and crucified you as they would a common criminal.

You arose from the dead. Many were witness to the fact. But before all of these things, you gathered around you men as your disciples, who were to go out into the world and communicate your teachings and truth to others. In the books that exist until this day, those teachings compose what we in the Christian world call the Bible.

With all of these things, however, whole civilizations have come and gone. Earthquakes have ravaged the land. Lands that were once barren are fruitful. Lands that were fruitful are barren. The seas have converged upon land in many diverse places, and lands have been reborn of the sea. Wars upon wars have been commonplace. In short, there has been a relentless destruction and rebirth of people, places, and things.

The aftermath to all this is that man has still been able to rise from the ashes of disease, pestilence, war, and other unsavory hosts. In my day, *technology* has become the key word. Things now in everyday use were unheard of when I was yet a boy. Medicine, industry, entertainment are all different. In closer scrutiny, they are only a rebirth or outgrowth from previously.

In our sciences, miracles are being performed, the likes of which were unknown to previous generations. We have cloning, atom smashing, powerful weapons that can both create or destroy, instruments with which we can scan the farthest regions of the universe or explore the innermost regions of our makeup.

In all of these things, I ask myself, "How is it possible that believers in you can continue to endure their tribulations by faith alone?" I call out daily. I hear no physical voice in my tongue in response. I look for you. But aside from my knowledge of your existence in all things, I don't see form in my image.

Nonetheless, I believe in you fervently. I believe you do communicate with me. It is present in my writings, my music, my thoughts, my long-suffering and patience. That is where I sense I see and hear you.

Grant me in closing, Lord, the humility and humbleness to remain steadfast in all my endeavors. Grant me the subliminal satisfaction that all I seek to achieve be accomplished. Endow me with a spirit of forgiveness for all those who would or do try my patience or afflict me with their stings of persecution. Help me to absorb all that is right and abhor all that would offend or destroy my will. In all of my endeavors, be they large or small, I pray that ultimately I will accomplish those purposes for which you have granted me life on this precious earth.

Amen.

Prescription for Life

(January 4, 1988)

Have you ever noticed the number of people who claim they have a prescription for longevity? Since I was a small boy, I have seen the passing parade of newspaper copy, magazine articles, and television interviews of people offering ideas ranging everywhere from drinking a cup of fresh blood each day to sexual abstinence.

Amid a veritable mountain of words heard in the country daily are such lead-in phrases as: "Do you want to live longer?"; "We can show you the way to a healthier, happier life"; and, "If you follow this advice, you will live to a ripe old age."

Promoters abound in wanting to convert people's living and eating habits to abstinence from smoking or drinking, giving up junk foods, and a host of other mind recommendations.

The paranoia attached to this blitz is mind-boggling. We are threatened that if we don't mend our ways, we will die tomorrow. Various religions have always promised "eternal life" if we adhere to certain precepts. Others testify that if we follow tenets of their faith we will not succumb to sickness or disease. For those adopting a more practical stance, it is our future life or spiritual life that is going to be enhanced.

The entire medical profession is dedicated to healing the sick and offering us a longer, healthier existence. Such is the main reason the general public has relegated doctors to a godlike posture. Aside from treating our infirmities, the real drawing power of the medical practitioners is their ability to extend life, via their prescriptions.

Health faddists abound. There are few cities where some practitioner is lacking in this area. Health food stores, self-appointed nutritional experts, health clubs, exercise parlors, you name it. They are everywhere. As if this weren't enough, we have manufacturers of all types of products advertising how theirs will indeed improve vitality and help us to live longer.

We mustn't forget dear old Mother. She is the prime source of all our early knowledge in life. Her expertise (real or imagined) is drummed into us long after we have a mind of our own and can reason for ourselves. "Eat this, darling, it's good for you"; "Don't go outside without your sweater, you'll catch your death of cold." Virtually all children have heard those two particular cautions.

Is all this bombardment confined to the United States? I doubt it. But we are in the forefront of this activity. Americans seem to be suffering a whole plethora of fears predicated solely on the concept that we can live forever if we eat the right things, take care of the body in the right way, exercise regularly, get enough sleep, don't put ourselves under any undue stress, watch out for accidents, don't play with matches, and on and on and on.

Let's be realistic. Most of our living concerns the fear of dying and the desire to prolong life. But there has been an additional amendment tacked onto the fear of dying. We should fear dying young. We must live longer.

A very wise prophet, Jesus, in fact, spoke to his disciples, saying, "It isn't what goes into the mouth that defileth the man, but what ushers forth from the mouth." I see those few words as sage. Do things in moderation.

Don't fret about them. Live them. Experience them. We were probably meant to experience so we could learn. Living a life of fear and reproach is much like living in a cave somewhere doing nothing. Trying to extend a natural life at the expense of all else is absurd.

If you believe in a nonphysical realm either before birth or after death, what is the sense in shackling yourself to prolong a physical existence?

In universal terms, regardless of years, all of us live a rather short span of life on earth. In my own life, prescriptions from doctors have changed as often as the weather. The public is being fed contradictory information on a regular basis. Things good for you today are reversed and labeled as bad tomorrow. The medical profession cannot seem to make up their minds.

To me, the real prescription for living is to give thanks when you wake up in the morning and find you can look forward to another day. Similarly, when you go to bed for the night you can give thanks you were able to experience all the day had to offer. Face up to the reality that quality of life deteriorates, like the quality of any product you buy as it ages. Live with that. Be happy about that. Be thankful you can eat, socialize with people, and have a place to rest your head.

This prescription may not extend your life, but it will provide you an inner tranquillity that has a special quality all its own.

Roman Numerals

(May 27, 1989)

Roman numerals annoy the hell out of me. So often I see them used following copyright notices or television programming, where the year is supposed to be articulated for some major or minor reason.

Who can honestly read them today? I feel reasonably convinced if you go into any public place and ask the first ten people you see to write the dates of their birth, their Social Security numbers, and their driver's license numbers all in Roman numerals, you will get ten wrong answers. Ask any one of the ten to write the Roman numeral for "zero"—a simple enough request, to be sure—but it's likely that 50 percent or better will be unable to do that either.

According to my dictionary, Roman numerals were in use only until the tenth century A.D. Express that year in Roman numerals if you would please! See what I mean?

Is there a law someplace stating they have to be used in today's world? Are outlines of writings, chapters of books, or acts of plays required to be listed in Roman numerals? If not, why use them? Does chapter XIX sound better than chapter 19? Is it easier for us to read or for the printer to set type? Of course not! Is an opera or a play better served by Act IV instead of the 4th Act? I doubt it seriously.

What then is our obsession? Why do certain divisions

within our society find Roman numerals appealing? Is something from before the tenth century trendy? Are we more impressed by someone using Roman numerals? Whatever the reason for whichever group uses them, I am annoyed.

Can you imagine some of the following things around us today expressed in Roman numerals? James Bond, Agent 007. The manufacturers' nomenclature of their product, for example, a Boeing 747. Timetables and twenty-four-hour clock times. Your zip code. Your telephone number. Any of your identification numbers. The amount of money you earn or owe toward the purchase of a house or automobile. Street numbers on signs. The numbers of minutes and seconds left in your favorite sport or the expiration date on a coupon. It would be a zany world indeed.

As for myself, I'd love to see Roman numerals eliminated entirely, excepting of course references to their use in the past in dictionaries or encyclopedias.

With the growing use of so many new symbols in our lives that need to be learned, I see no gain in catering to and keeping around Roman numerals.

Save, Win, Success

(November 13, 1974)

Some of the more unobtrusive evils in this society today are contained in advertising slogans beamed daily on the various channels of our television sets. You've seen them by the score. But aside from brushing many of them off initially for what they are, many of us succumb to their message. That, of course, is what advertising is all about.

Of what I consider to be the three most prominent messages broadcast through this medium, none produces what it promises. Let's look at the three:

First, there is the save message. This will be vocalized in a million different tones. It will be orchestrated by language, color, and sound. The message is there. The point is profound. You can save. But it is always a lie! You do not save. You spend! And that is the intent of the advertising message. You must go out now—tonight or tomorrow—to spend. If you spend, you will save. Of course, you never save when you spend. You save when you don't spend. It's that simple. Far too many people raised in the era of dramatic advertising believe they are saving. They are not. They are spending. This might be why so many children find it difficult to save. Hearing thousands of such commercial messages, they think that saving means rushing out and buying something. Saving means rushing out to the bank with coins, bills, or checks and banking them in an account under your name without withdrawing the money. That is saving.

Second, there is the "you'll win this" or "you'll win that" routine. This message appears visibly and vocally, much the same as the save mentality messages. It is also a lie! You don't win; you buy. And however you examine it, what you think you have won is a deceit. It is most likely (and more truthfully) something you bought. If it wasn't something you bought, it was something they induced you to enter so your name could be used to have others sell you. In the field of advertising, this type of selling practice is common. The claim that you will win is strictly hype.

Third, we have the important message brought to you directly or subliminally of how important it is to be successful. These claims of how they define success mean that you have appeal; you look and act the way the proprietors want you to act. An old musical commercial is typical. "You look sharp, feel sharp—da-di-da-di-dah!" Clothes, cosmetics, salves, soaps, and even suppositories, to mention a few, are all sold with the underlying road-to-success stories. They appeal to your ego. They imply, by virtue of their claims, that you, too, can enjoy all the qualities they are displaying and thus be better—be successful.

Don't believe it. These too are lies. Success is a misnomer. It doesn't mean the same thing to everyone. It, in the vernacular of these messages, means that you'll do as they want you to do. And what they want you to do is buy their product.

In the beginning of this commentary, I used the word "evil." It is threatening to cause one to believe something when the belief is intended to foster something else. Believing to save when you must spend is not saving at all. That is a threat. It is a threat to your pocketbook. It is even more of a threat to your power of reasoning. In fact,

126

it may even inhibit your deductive powers as well. It is a threat to have you think you can win when the odds are likened unto the odds of being struck by a bolt of lightning. This form of reasoning is also an attack of the mind. It is alien to good mentality. Lotteries with odds approaching 25 million to 1 are a good example of this form of threat.

To imply success is attained by virtue of looks, smell, affiliation, size, shape, type of clothes, and so on, is absolutely ridiculous. Success is not easily measured because it implies results of a favorable nature to the beholder, rather than any degree of attainment to the holder. In the former, one is given to believe a lie. In the latter, it is more often a statement of fact.

Again, as with the other two messages, we see that the method is opposed to rational thinking. In all three instances, the threats I have mentioned are more than just a threat. They are a veritable rape of our minds.

Semantics comes into play in all of the above words— save, win, success. Because you believe or want to believe you can save. Or because you believe or want to believe you can win. Or because you believe or want to believe you will be a success, the perpetrator of the advertising message gets through to you. They rely on the knowledge you will believe what you want to believe. And if they can formulate their message to mold your thinking, you will act accordingly.

Those three monkeys on our backs (save, win, success) extend far beyond the simple, platonic appearance any offer on television suggests. What is the real importance of saving? Save our souls, maybe! Save our children, of course! Save our country and its principles, without doubt. Save some reserves financially to protect from an unforeseen calamity, absolutely. But where are the savings so vital to our lives that we must rush out and spend? And quite often driving far out of our way to do so.

Winning is important, too. But what if we lost? Is that a crime? Is that a catastrophe? I think honestly I have learned far more from losing than I have from winning. I have made more friends of losers than winners, found more desire to improve myself from losing than from winning. I've learned to be humble. I've learned how to be gracious. I set about more changes in my life for the better from losing. Winning, as I see it, fosters haughtiness, conceit, jealousy, condemnation of others, a caste mentality, and prudishness and makes one a potential target for freeloaders, exploiters, and even criminals.

Success, though important, can and does have its drawbacks. It strains credibility. Who is to say that because I am not rich I am not successful? Who is so bold as to suggest if I don't conform to established criteria I am not going to be successful? Am I a failure if my personal views and habits do not conform with their images? Or their marketing and advertising ploys?

It would serve you well to remember the next time you are so comfortably seated in front of your television that "advertising does sell," however objectionable you think it is. And it does more than sell. It conditions your mind to act and react in a manner befitting of their goals. Give pause to reflect on what messages are being beamed into your mind. I have only mentioned three obvious methods (save, win, success). There are others.

Space

(April 29, 1986)

I never cease to be amazed at the immensity of the heavens. Each night, when I step outside my home and gaze skyward, I am confronted with planets, stars, and constellations. Some I know, from having learned about them. Others are merely points of light in space.

What amazes me most is the incredible distances (by our measuring stick, the sun) we can see with our naked eyes. None of us could travel to any of those points in a lifetime. The speed of light is beyond comprehension as it is—186,000 miles per second. To think what appears before us each evening is beyond reach at even that phenomenal speed is, to say the very least, quite humbling.

Our egos somehow restrict us in good measure. More than our mind, it is the ego that hampers understanding. I rather suspect if we could conquer our egos, many of life's mysteries would be more readily comprehensible.

Tonight, as so many nights before, I wished. I prayed. I tried to open my mind to the immensity. Surely, with all that was visible before me, there was something to be learned, something beneficial I could derive. And indeed there was.

Imagine yourself as one of the millions of microscopic life-forms in the ocean. You have eyes to see. You have sensors to probe into the reaches of your environment.

What do you see? You may see the floor of the ocean in the shallows. You may see other life similar to yourself. You certainly will see enemies, compatriots, and a variety of food sources and scenery. What you most likely will not see is what lies beyond that ocean in which you dwell.

For all practical purposes, that ocean is to the microscopic life-forms no different from the heaven we gaze into at night. It is our universe, as indeed the ocean may be to its life-forms. As they most apparently cannot comprehend what is beyond the ocean, we cannot comprehend anything different beyond the mighty universe than what our instruments can detect.

Philosophically, I have learned one basic truth about man's relationship with his known world. Whether it be inward or outward, contracted or expanded, he is occupying a space not too much different from all he sees. In other words, he may be a giant to microscopic life. He conversely is microscopic himself in yet a bigger world.

Jonathan Swift, in his book *Gulliver's Travels,* pointed this out to us quite eloquently. I might diverge a moment to mention he pointed out far more truths in his book than are generally recognized by the public to this day.

Nonetheless, if we can accept these examples as an insight to expanding our minds, then a greater awareness must surely present itself in the future. That expanse of sky that we loosely refer to as the heaven is no more than our ocean. It is something contained in something much bigger. And yet, who is to say, it might be as a drop of water to an even greater entity.

Along with that reality of thinking, I must note something that I believe enters into everyone's mind during their lifetime. We all like to think the answers to mysteries we don't receive in this life will be miraculously revealed upon our death. My cognitive desire is like yours. However, in dwelling upon the matter, I don't think it is logical. I rather believe death is not a panacea to understanding. It, most likely, is a stepping-stone into future experiences that hone us into greater reality—some new reality in space.

The Spoken Word

(April 19, 1989)

In one of our recent discussions, my daughter, Sheryl, told me she had evidenced a great change in her life by saying her prayers out loud. In this very same discussion, she was somewhat shocked to hear some of my personal beliefs about prayer—especially that I felt guilty in asking for help or assistance in those things I was capable of doing for myself. In my reasoning, I feel we have been endowed with a brain, eyes, ears, nose, arms, legs, and hands—all good tools for problem solving. Why then should we burden God with prayers reciting our personal problems?

In suggesting that I consider praying out loud, I acknowledged I would do so from time to time and report back to her about my thoughts or experiences on the matter.

My first such prayer, two nights ago, found me talking to God and affirming my belief that thoughts are a silent communication, that my music is an intonement of prayer—a voice of a different kind, but nonetheless a communication. Physical action is likewise a communion with God. I refer to this action as a physical prayer. Why then the necessity for vocalizing things already expressed in other terms?

Referring back to my conversation with Sheryl, I restated an observation I had made to her: "When I read my writings aloud, it helped to improve them." In that statement, I realized there was a glimmer of understanding I might learn something more about the spoken word.

It has always been my contention the dictionary is our most beneficial and valuable book. So I took my *Webster's New World Dictionary* from the shelf and began reading. To my surprise, thirty-seven pages were dedicated to its understanding before a single word was listed. On page 31, under "Etymology," or the study of the origin and development of words, I was further surprised to read the following: "The Greeks, like much earlier primitive man, sensed a mysterious relationship between the word and that for which it stands. To know how to pronounce the word correctly could give the user power over the thing or being, a principle of great importance in the exercise of witchcraft. But conversely, it could also be dangerous to pronounce the names of certain beings, for to do so might arouse the anger of the immanent spirit . . ."

The spoken word moves people; of that there is little doubt. Orators, elocutionists, prophets, and martyrs have provided history with an abundance of examples—sadly, not all for good. We do see from this a preponderance of evidence that the utterances from one's mouth or tongue support the biblical reference that it is the tongue that defileth a man. This implies the tongue, which formulates words and utterances, can do harm.

Getting back to the power of the spoken word, I recognize that wizards, witches, and sorcerers all used incantations of the spoken word to create magic. They exercised powers common men found baffling. Was the invoking of such power solely by the spoken word?

Jesus, in his role as teacher and healer, did not invoke power. He *was* power. He was the physical personification of God the Father. There was no need to summon it. He merely laid his hands upon the sick and afflicted, then commanded them to go forth and resume their lives.

I feel intuitively, however, he would have summoned

the Holy Ghost, as indeed upon his death he uttered the phrase, "Eli, Eli, lama sabach thani?" This has been interpreted to mean, "My God, my God, why hast thou forsaken me?" I do not agree with that interpretation at all. I perceive the phrase to be one in a tongue from space or long-forgotten language on earth suggesting he was asking, "Enough, enough, already. Isn't it time for me to return, Father?" He was ready to commend his spirit back to God.

The Bible, the Book of Science and Health, and the Diaclot all teach us to pray in silence. We are instructed not to be like the hypocrites and Pharisees, who enjoy listening to themselves and seek the vain adulation of others.

I still hold fast to my belief that prayer is better voiced in silence through meditation. I am of the belief also that man has a unique gift, not only to think and reason, but to orally express those ideas. Inflections, cadence, pronunciation, and assemblage of words release varying amounts of energy. Chants, commands, orders, and curses prove this reasoning.

Chants raise the vibratory factors in people to send and receive spiritual consciousness. Commands and orders invoke conditional responses to authority that can have a paralyzing, hypnotic effect. Anger and emotional curses vented from our body release chemical reagents by electroshock waves, which largely overpower reason and objectivity.

Jesus, in his infinite wisdom, realizing the tremendous power of the spoken word, suggested we would be better served by silent prayer. I think I'll conclude the same.

Victory over Defeat

(March 15, 1988)

An interesting question coursed through my mind late this afternoon as the result of a very difficult day. Either God loves me a great deal and is testing me for my conviction and courage or the Devil hates me immensely and is throwing a barrage of misfortune my way, in attempts to undermine my stamina. Which is the more correct?

The answer may be none of the above. From my understanding, it can be both.

In the laws of physics, there is one law that states, "For every action, there is an equal or opposing reaction." This would serve to explain a good deal about my rationalization. To me, the beauty of so many of our scientific laws is that they characterize and paint a picture of the entity we commonly consider God.

More than faith alone, more than doctrine, more than idiomatic expressions or biblical nuances, I think scientific realities point to the verity of a supreme force regulating our world and universe. Call it what you will, this goes a long way toward defining that nebulous entity so many of the world's peoples call God.

Deeds of good and benevolence have always been ascribed to God. The negativity, the selfishness, and the evils of the world have always been ascribed to the Devil. It is no wonder that my opening question was a good one.

Which of the two personages could be attributed to the many difficulties prevalent in my life today?

Only this afternoon, street hoodlums shot out the rear window of my 1972 Ambassador station wagon. This incident was another in a long string of unfortunate happenings since I decided to have the car refurbished. Joined together with many other pressing problems in my life—namely, severe angina and limited physical mobility—it was very hard for me. Such an incident may seem innocuous enough, but the extraordinary details involved to correct the incident rob one of precious time, energy, and other projects.

Most agnostics would laugh at the mere suggestion some opposing force was behind today's episode. But they do not recognize a basic fact: nothing happens in this world except that it is the motivation of some force. If you were going through the first grade of school, it might be too difficult to grasp. Each progressive grade level brings about a new awareness by education and experience. In order to gain promotion to a higher level, achievement tests are given to determine individual capability.

Take the military, for example, rather than the more mundane school. Leadership ability, emotional stability, and reaction to various situations under stress are but a few of the factors that are evaluated by military personnel before promotions are awarded. At all levels of responsibility, regardless of profession, people are tested again and again to determine if they are qualified for the position being considered.

In this light, I consider my recent problems as tests of a sort. Am I stable? Am I strong enough to weather the formidable host of circumstances foisted upon me in order to make something worthwhile of my continued living? Those are good questions.

Looking at it another way, we can imagine an opposing force would attempt to wear down a person's resolve. It is the essence of war. This is the very foundation of attack. Demoralize your enemy. Weaken their position. Blast away at their fortifications. Feed them propaganda to disrupt their convictions.

Patience, fortitude, courage, endurance, and moral convictions are but a very few of the standards by which any entity must employ to hold firm in the face of opposition. And it is just such tools I try to keep in my inventory to promote victory over defeat.

What about Your House?

(October 13, 1990)

During a period of reflection today, it occurred to me many of the rooms around my home bore names or references that were completely erroneous or nondescriptive of the real activity and use we have made of them. I had to laugh to myself, wondering if Andy Rooney's place was the same.

To begin, our garden court at the entrance to our house is neither a garden in the real sense nor a court by any of the fifteen definitions shown in *Webster's Ninth New Dictionary. Courtyard* comes closest to defining what it is: "A court or enclosure adjacent to a building (as a house or place)." Again, however, it is quite inaccurate, since neither of the words *court* or *yard* are applicable. So, what is it? In looking further in the dictionary, I see the word *patio* says it is a "courtyard—especially an inner court open to the sky." Why wasn't that definition shown earlier under "courtyard" itself? Well, for all practical purposes I suppose we could describe our courtyard as a "patiocourt."

Upon entering the house, the first room visible to anyone is the living room. Everybody has a living room. We all know what it is, don't we? In ours, however, it is a dying room! No one goes there save at Christmas, when a gaily decorated pine or spruce tree is placed there and festooned with multicolored lights. Once in a blue moon, some company will join us and we'll sit around socially, but like cold and frigid people, stiff and uncomfortable!

The furniture—tables, sofas, chairs, wall decorations, etc.—are basically ornamentations set out on display like in a museum. It would be better to label this room a display room, a museum room, a hollow room—almost anything but a living room. There is virtually no living done in that room.

Next to this is our den, one of the more frequented rooms in the house. But is it a den? It's not a lair of any wild animal. It's not a hollow cavern or cave used as a hideout. It's not the center of any secret activity. It's not the subdivision of a Cub Scout pack. It's definitely not a small, squalid dwelling. But the final definition comes closest when it says: "A comfortable secluded room." Ours is far from *secluded.* It is, in a way, an extension of our kitchen without being shuttered or enclosed by doors. As such, it doesn't fit the definition of the name ascribed to it. Call it a lounging room maybe, a television room perhaps. Both would be more correct.

Our kitchen is definitely a kitchen and then some. It is in my opinion the center of our family structure. We communicate there. We entertain there. We socialize there. We play games there. We read our newspapers and magazines there. Most of our letter writing is done there. In fact, the kitchen table serves as an ironing board, a drafting and cutting table, a packing and shipping department, a repair bench, a game table, an office desk, and a dining table all wrapped up in one. This room should be more correctly referred to as the living kitchen.

A hallway is a corridor, but I wouldn't tell a visitor who asked, "Where is the bathroom?" to "go down to the end of the carpeted corridor, turn right, and it's the first door to your right." We most probably and do say, "Go down to the end of the hall. It's the first door on your right."

Does the visitor go down? Good grief, don't ask my wife Penny that question!

Everyone uses the bathroom, but it's seldom for a bath! Enough said about that!

Our home is a four-bedroom house, but you'd be hard pressed to find them. You could find an office, a music room, a sewing room, but four bedrooms—forget it.

Why is it we stick to the superficial names passed down from generations before us that have been applied to these rooms? Is it out of laziness or sham? Is it because of some unwillingness to change? We all know that we fight change more than anything else in our lives. I suppose the answer may be found in our garage. It is rarely a garage. It could be called a warehouse for storing what doesn't fit in the house. It could be called a junk heap or a trash bin, both being more truthful.

We call it a garage because that is what everyone else calls it.

Why Does Man Examine Life?

(November 27, 1988)

What is there about life that prompts man to seek its definition? Or search for plausible meaning? We compare it, try to shape it, look for it elsewhere in the universe, and examine it in the most hidden places and minutest forms.

In looking to the heavens as I do so often, I am somewhat of the opinion that we have been programmed from ages past to do precisely what we are doing. We have spent generations of time arriving (thanks to centuries of education) at the realization that we must leave this planet someday for our survival and/or salvation.

Man has always been fixed with an admiration for earth, although it is not matched by his respect or appreciation of it. So far as has been discovered, there is nothing else in the known universe approaching earth's beauty. Man, nonetheless, has a deep desire to journey into space. It matters little what educational background people have, nor how advanced they have become, technically speaking. The lure and lore of the heavens are inescapable. Is this because the heavens are a master receptacle for the DNA of our civilization? The DNA chain is found in all forms of life. If such is found to be the case, then we can speak in other terms to say it has been ordained. And certainly there seems to be growing evidence life may not have had its beginnings on earth.

Such beginnings may have originated elsewhere in the universe.

Stories abound about "aliens." In trying to establish some measure of understanding about this curious interest, I call your attention to ancient manuscripts, biblical history, comic book characters, and more recently the UFO phenomena. In them we find a common thread. The world is looking for a Messiah. The advent of "Superman" in the late 1930s and the current ongoing mystery of "flying saucers," which began in the late 1940s, emphasize the point.

To me, there is no doubt man has some extended branches in the heavens. Do you believe that? Well, think about this for a moment. With all of our marvelous network of sensors—be they telescopes, radar equipment, etc.—man has not been able to define life as we know it elsewhere in the heavens. In that context, we are alone on a magnificent blue planet viewing the expanding universe. But are we really alone?

Gaze at the heavens regularly as I do. Sooner or later you'll see a "shooting star." Naturally, we have learned this is in reality a meteor, a fragment of something from elsewhere in space. It could be remnants from the well-publicized asteroid belt, which in Bode's mathematical laws had to have been a planetary body lying between Mars and Jupiter.

Additionally, at various times we have observed comets. The theory of today postulates that comets circle our sun in huge elliptical orbits, returning at precise intervals. Their effect on earth is only now beginning to be understood. In the "Gala Theory," comets have had an enormous impact upon earth, possibly responsible for life and, most assuredly, the demise of the dinosaurs.

Daily the spent remains of meteors, known as

meteorites, strike the earth. Those alien bodies have become a part of earth. What did they bring besides their basic composition of nickel and other metals? Have we been able to say nothing?

What I am trying to say here is three things: 1) We have a programmed interest in looking to the heavens and escaping the bonds of earth at some time in the future. 2) The known penetration of a foreign body through our atmosphere is logical enough to surmise that other forms of matter have done likewise. They may have, in fact, contributed to and become a part of our society without our awareness. 3) If some contributing factor in our society has arrived in that manner, there is no reason for us to believe we cannot escape and migrate elsewhere.

As far-fetched as it might seem, our inescapable fascination with the universe may be the direct result of "space debris" from meteors and comets. If you believe this is an absurd concept and nothing happens from that heavenly activity, just think about the bombardment of atoms and molecules from protons, ions, and antimatter. Here there is ample evidence that changes of enormous proportions do occur. I believe the example is sage. As man evolves, he is compelled to examine life in every recess of the known world. And, for that matter, the unknown world also.